HUNGARY

The Hungarians, or Magyars, reached their present homeland in the Carpathian Basin around 896 A.D. There had been other peoples here before the Magyars, and like them, they led semi-nomadic lives, but they were swept away by the storms of history. The Magyars were the only people who succeeded in creatury a nation and a home for themselves in the region. This success was in part due to the realization that they could survive as a nation not by opposing the rest of Europe, but by forging close ties with it. This was also the ideology that inspired Prince Géza and his son, the later King (Saint) Stephen and their descendants. For centuries they were thus able to protect Hungary's sovereignty, striving to adopt from Europe those things which were beneficial, and without detriment to national identity. By the Middle Ages Hungary had become one of the great powers of the region, but in the 16th century it was overrun by Ottoman Turks. For 150 years the country became the scene of a succession of wars, which decimated its people, depleted its wealth, and slowed its progress and development.

After the Turks were driven from the land, Hungary became part of the Habsburg Empire, but the power politics of the Court of Vienna limited the country's rehabilitation. In response, the leading political and cultural figures wanted to ensure the constitutional independence of the nation within the Empire. The clash of interests led to the revolution of 1848-1849 and to Europe's longest struggle for freedom, eventually put down by the great powers – the Habsburg Empire and Russia – joining forces. After the 1867 Compromise with the House of Habsburg, however, Hungary began an unprecedented period of economic and cultural development, especially in the fields of science and the arts.

The First World War slowed down the rate of development, but Hungary survived, despite being deprived of two-thirds of its territory and one-third of its people. After the catastrophe of the Second World War, Hungary became a Soviet satellite, but its people could still not be broken, as evidenced by the revolution and freedom fights of 1956, the first serious blow to the Communist world order.

After the change to a democratic regime in 1990, Hungary was once again able to return to the path of co-operation with Europe. Today it is proud of its forefathers for having defended the nation's sovereignty, and of the cultural achievements with which it was able to enrich European culture as a whole.

1

2

1. The Royal Castle atop Castle Hill in Buda, with the medieval Mace Tower and the Grand Rondella, and the Church of Tabán in the foreground.
2. The Hotel Hilton, built upon the ruins of an ancient Dominican monastery, with the towers of the Fishermen's Bastion in the foreground.
3. Equestrian statue of St. Stephen, the founder of the state, situated on Trinity Square in the Castle District.

BUDAPEST

3

The neo-gothic Parliament, built at the
turn of the 19th and 20th centuries,
looks across the Danube as proudly as ever.
Across from it rises Castle Hill with the Buda Hills
as its backdrop. As far as we know,
this was the first inhabited area, in what is now
Budapest, with people living
in its sandstone caves many centuries ago.
According to legend, the ancient Gauls fled
to nearby Aquincum from Troy.
It is not a legend, but plain fact, however, that
Aquincum – part of today's Óbuda – became
the most important city of the Roman province
of Pannonia. After the Mongolian invasion of
1241-42, the royal seat was moved to Castle Hill
in Buda.
The center of the occupying Turkish forces was also
the Castle of Buda. After the expulsion
of the Turks, hardly any Hungarian was spoken
across the river, in the newly rebuilt Pest.
With time the however commercial and
industrial development which is necessary
to the growth of any big city became centered
in Pest. Budapest, which by the early
18th century had acquired this name,
was actually born only in 1873 with the
unification of Pest, Buda and Óbuda.
The capital, which had a population of
nearly two million, also moved its political
and administrative centers to the flat cityscope
of Pest.

4

4. *The stone steeples and towers of Matthias Church and the Fishermen's Bastion in the Castle District.*
5. *Fortuna Street.*
6-8. *Old house façades in the Castle District, a mélange of gothic, baroque and Louis XVI. style.*

5

6

7

8

9. *The neo-gothic Parliament building on the Pest bank of the Danube*
10. *The Chain Bridge, the oldest bridge in Budapest.*
11. *Towers of the baroque Church of St. Anne, with Margaret Bridge in the background.*

12. *The Klotild Palace, one of the most beautiful art nouveau buildings of Pest's Inner City.*
13. *Neo-baroque caryatids on Andrássy Street.*
14. *Warm-water pond on Margaret Island.*
15. *The Castle of Vajdahunyad with the City Park lake, built for the 1906 World Fair.*

11

12

14

15

13

16

17   18

8

THE DANUBE BEND

On its long, winding journey from the
Black Forest to the Black Sea, the Danube
first slows down, becoming wider and parting to
form small islands, just downstream of Vienna,
on Hungary's Kisalföld, or Small Plain.
But soon its width is once again restricted by
mountains, and only having skirted the
Pilis Mountains and forests and making
a sharp turn to the south, can it flow at a leisurely
pace once again. One-thousand years ago, when
the nation was founded, and the
Hungarian kingdom was established,
the nation's axis of power was a
line between the towns of Székesfehérvár to the
south and Esztergom to the north.
The dense Pilis woodlands, an ideal refuge
from attack, was very close by. The royal seat was
transferred from Esztergom,
the largest town only much later on the Danube
Bend, to Buda, lying at the lower end of the
great bend. For a long time,
on both sides of the bend, the Danube
was blessed with rich orchards. Some time ago,
though, the trees were replaced by houses
and summer homes, until the settlements have
practically merged into each other – on the right
bank from Esztergom to Budapest, and
on the left from Vác to Budapest.

19

16. *Szentendre is known for its Serb-Orthodox churches.*
Its hilly, winding streets, ancient squares and alleys conjure up
the mood of a small Mediterranean town.
17. *The Parish Church, built on medieval foundations,*
rises above Szentendre's Main Square.
18. *A narrow alley, one of several, conjures up times long-past.*
19. *Old merchants' houses on Szentendre's main street.*

THE DANUBE BEND

20. *The Upper Castle of Visegrád
dates back to the 1250s.*
21. *The gothic arcades of the
15th century palace of Visegrád,
built for King Matthias.*
22-24. *The 15th century renaissance fountain
carved from red marble in the courtyard
of the palace of Visegrád.
Details of the so-called Lion Well
and the marble fountain.*

11

25

27

12

25. *The 19th century neo-classical Basilica of Esztergom.*
26. *A service in the Basilica.*
27. *A 14th century fresco in the palace chapel.*
28. *The royal palace of Esztergom built in the 1220s.*
29. *Decorated and carved capital in the palace chapel.*

26

28   29

THE DANUBE BEND

32

NORTHERN HUNGARY

The chain of mountains made up of
the Börzsöny, Cserhát, Mátra, Bükk, Zemplén and
Tokaj ranges north-east from
the Danube Bend. Together they form a chain,
but each has its distinctive physical features,
and different groups of people pursuing
different trades and professions.
There are no really high mountain peaks.
The highest, situated at Kékes in the Mátra,
is only 1,015 meters. Kékes and the other taller,
more regal mountain peaks are surrounded
by their more modest partners the way a grand
lord is surrounded by an entourage.
For centuries, most of the people living
among these mountains made a living cultivating
flat areas of the region. But in addition there was
forestry, wood-working, lime and charcoal
burning, and there were mines-some of
which are still open today. Most of them,
however, are no longer being dug any deeper
into the scarred earth. The exhausted,
abandoned mines and quarries of the mountains
became known for the beautiful colors of their
crystal formations, known as "mine flowers", and
prized by collectors of minerals.

30. *Landscape from Northern Hungary.*
31-32. *Lippican horses at Szilvásvárad.*

33-35. *The wooden-towered church and peasant houses of Hollókő, which has preserved its folk architecture and is today a World Heritage Site.*

34

33

35

36-38. *The church of Csaroda is a combination of Romanesque-age and folk architecture. Inside, on its northern wall, remnants of a 13th century wall painting have survived.*
39. *In Rimóc, which lies near Hollókő surrounded by beautiful mountains, people still wear their traditional folk costumes.*

38

36

39

37

40

41

42

43

NORTHERN HUNGARY

40. *View of Eger.*
41. *The castle of Eger.*
42. *Gothic corridor in the castle of Eger.*
43. *Baroque niche in Eger's town center.*
44-45. *Main façade of the Basilica of Eger.*
46. *Fresco on the ceiling of the library of Eger's old Líceum (secondary school for girls).*

47. *Lillafüred's Castle Hotel was never a castle at all. It was built in the 1930s as a luxury hotel.*
48-49. *Tokay-Hegyalja and environs are famous for their excellent wines.*

49

47

48

52

50

51

50-52. *Details of the Rákóczy family castle.*
in Sárospatak and the 16th century renaissance staircase in
the inner courtyard.

53

54

53-54. The people of the Hortobágy puszta near Debrecen still breed animals in the ancient way. In order to preserve Hortobágy and Apaj pusztas as "living museums", both have been turned into National Parks.
55-56. The best sheep dogs in Hungary are the komondor and the puli.

22

THE GREAT PLAIN

The Great Plain underwent a tremendous transformation during the 20th century. Farms disappeared, while the size of villages and towns doubled. In one place a forest belt was planted, in another forests were cut down. In one place the water of a fish pond gleams in the sun, in another there is nothing left but a dried-out bed. To this day, the Great Plain must make its changes with an eye to the existence of some nearby source of water. Nature, too, transformed the Great Plain throughout the 19th century.

The decrease in forests, higher winds, the puszta use for agriculture, all brought major changes. But it took the regulation of the waters, especially the River Tisza in the 19th century, to put an end to the Tisza's period flooding of the flatlands, when the only means of transportation was by boat, and people had to leave their homes. Today on the other hand, frequent droughts destroy plowlands and disrupt the local economy.

Luckily, even so, the Great Plain has remained a huge "pantry" despite all this. Its wheat is hardy, its paprika is "sweet and noble", the aroma of its fruits and vegetables are incomparable. The Great Plain is also known throughout the world for its natural endowments and the untouched beauty of what is left of its pusztas.

55

56

57

59

60

57. *Horse-herds on the Hortobágy in traditional costume.*
58. *A famous stud, or ménes, of the Hortobágy.*
59-60. *Gray cattle, distinquished by their long horns and robust build, are indiginous to the Hortobágy.*

25

61. *Debrecen, whose speedy development turned it into a modern town. In the foreground is the so-called Great Church of Debrecen.*
62. *View of the Great Plain.*
63. *Kecskemét is the principal town of Hungarian art nouveau.*
64. *The Cifra (Ornate) Palace of Kecskemét is one of the most beautiful examples of Hungarian art nouveau architecture.*
65. *The restored synagogue of Kecskemét.*

64

65

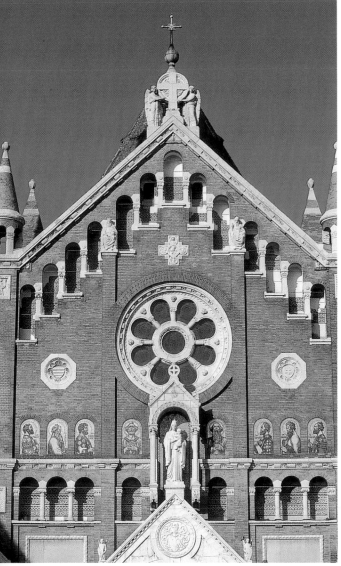

66

67

68

66. *Detail of the façade of the neo-romanesque Votive Church of Szeged.*
67. *Szeged Town Hall.*
68. *The Ferenc Móra Museum in Szeged.*
69.*Art nouveau residential building in Szeged town center.*
70. *Storks no longer nest atop the roofs of peasant houses.*
71. *The River Tisza.*

72

73

72. *Sailing is still the most popular sport on the lake.*
73. *The picturesque chain of hills of the Upper Balaton region.*
74. *The famous thermal hot-water lake of Hévíz.*
75. *The shallow, warm waters of the southern shore draw bathers by the thousands.*

BALATON AND ITS SURROUNDINGS

Geologically and hydrologically speaking, the Balaton, the largest lake of Central Europe, is way past its infancy. It has seen much, but has retained its attraction. The present surface of the lake, whose 600 square kilometer expanse of water gleams in the sunlight, was once almost twice as big. It is a shallow lake with on average depth of only 3 meters, and even below the Tihany Peninsula, the seat of a bishopric, it does not go deeper than 11.5 meters. This is why the lake is quick to warm up, and why, during summer storms, the wind whipping in from the Bakony Mountains turns the surface into a furious melée of ripping waves.

What had been so soft, gentle, and tranquil, turns in the twinkling of an eye into something deadly. The surrounding settlements, all resort areas, have in the meantime formed an almost continuous ring around the lake.

The Upper Balaton is not only extravagantly lovely, housing a whole gallery of unusual geological formations, but is also a first-rate wine region, and is rich in thermal waters, too.

74

75

77

76. The crypt of the Abbey Church of Tihany Peninsula dates from the 11th century. Tihany itself is one of the most popular resorts on the Balaton.
77. Farmhouse built in the peasant-baroque style in Badacsony.
78. One of the famous Badacsony vineyards.
79. A typical porched peasant house in the Upper Balaton region.
80. Press house in the Upper Balaton region.

BALATON AND ITS SURROUNDING

78

79

80

33

81. *The Festetich Palace, built by the Festetics family in 1745, has been turned into a beautiful museum.*
82-84. *Rooms inside the Festetich Palace.*
85. *The library of the Festetich Palace.*

BALATON AND ITS SURROUNDING

85

86. *Statues of King Saint Stephen, the founder of the nation, and his wife, Gizella of Bavaria, on the Castle Hill of Veszprém.*
87. *Veszprém, which lies on five hills just 10 kilometers from Lake Balaton, is one of the oldest towns in Hungary.*
88. *The town center of Székesfehérvár.*
89. *A 2nd century tombstone at the outdoor museum of Tác.*
90. *The main square of Székesfehérvár with the baroque bishop's palace on the right and the baroque Cistercian Church on the left.*

87

90

91

92

93

TRANSDANUBIA

Transdanubia is a small country in its own right. Its flatlands are made up of the Small Plain, while its hilly regions form a wide circle around the medium-high mountains, including the Bakony, the most beautiful of them all. At its foot lies Lake Balaton. The region's warm weather is tempered from the west by the nearby Alps, while its winters are made milder by the Mediterranean Sea. Perhaps the best way to describe the region is to say that it is gentle. This may be due to the soft, feminine curves of its boughs, as the poets insist. It has also retained something of its heritage from the Romans, who were here for nearly half a century, and called the entire region the province of Pannonia. To this day, the major influence on its cultural climate is its proximity to Western Europe. Southern Slavs and German-speaking populations settled the region, mingling with the Hungarians. The new impetus given to its old industries has also added to the prosperity of Transdanubia, thereby making it possible for the buildings of its beautiful old towns to have weathered the storms of history.

94

91. *The Abbey of Pannonhalma, founded in 1001.*
92. *The Porta Speciosa, the main entrance to the church, leads to the church via the cloister.*
93. *The gothic cloister of the abbey.*
94. *The Romanesque crypt of the abbey.*

97

95-96. *The Abbey Church of Ják, consecrated in1256, is one of the most beautiful Romanesque buildings to have survived in Hungary.*

97-98. *The interior of the 13th century Church of Velemér is decorated with frescoes from 1378.*

99. *A peasant house with a thatched roof in the Őrség, stands as a reminder of the folk architecture of the past.*

100. *Field-work in the Őrség.*

98

101. *The Barbican of Pécs is what's left of the medieval town fortifications.*
102. *Detail of the beautiful Zsolnai Fountain in Pécs.*
103. *The so-called Djami is among the most important buildings to have remained from the time of the Turkish Occupation.*
104-106. *The neo-Romanesque cathedral of Pécs.*
107. *Traditional end-of-winter masquarade, called the "Farsang".*
108. *Rows of press-houses in Villány.*

102

103

TRANSDANUBIA

109. *Detail of the Maria Column in Győr's Széchenyi Square.*
110. *The baroque Abbot House is today a museum.*
111. *The main shopping street in the inner city of Győr, with one of the Danube bridges in the background.*

112.-114. *The Esterházy Palace of Fertőd is the most beautiful baroque-rococo building in Hungary. It gained its present form in the 18th century.*

113

114

115. *An 18th century merchant's house in Sopron.*
116. *Old dwelling houses line the streets of Sopron's inner city.*
117. *The Fire Tower has become the symbol of Sopron.*
118. *The courtyard of Sopron's Storno House, now a museum.*
119. *Új Street in Sopron, with a beautifully restored gothic house in the foreground.*

115

117

116

118

120. *The 15th century Town Hall of Kőszeg.*
121. *The so-called Heroes' Gate on Kőszeg's main square.*

TRANSDANUBIA

Published by Magyar Könyvklub, Budapest, 2001
Printed by Reálszisztéma Dabasi Nyomda Rt.

ISBN 963 547 386 9